The Friend "Ly" Forest

An American Adventure in Adverbs and Adjectives

Dr. Richard U. Ly and Brandon D. Ly

First Edition

ISBN 978-1-961225-58-9 (paperback)
ISBN 978-1-961225-59-6 (hardback)
ISBN 978-1-961225-51-0 (digital)

Printed in the United States of America

Dads/Grandpas—Ve-Dan Ly and Uncle Bob
Moms/Grandmas—Linh Dao Ly, Lam Nga Dao, and Rosanna Lau
Cool Uncle Richard Stokes
Dear friend Donna Aliperti
Inspiration—Ainsley and Hayden Earhardt and Christina Kulhner
Our puppies—Muffin, Brownie, and Kinnoli (Nikki)

Contents

Chapter 1

Devoted Ly, the Dog

Devoted Ly is a great dog, a loyal friend, and an amazing companion. Years ago, she met her best friend Rich Ly, the rabbit, in a Merry Land far, far away. When they first met, Rich wasn't very nice to Devoted because they met under less-than-ideal circumstances. She was suddenly dropped off at Rich's doorstep, so he felt compelled to take care of her. It was a huge responsibility for Rich, who could barely take care of himself at that point in his life. On the other hand, meeting Rich changed everything for Devoted. She knew immediately she had a friend for life and was completely dedicated to her new friend. Unfortunately, Rich initially didn't reciprocate Devoted's love and affection. But in spite of how he treated her, she followed Rich around, devotedly. At first, he took her love and devotion for granted, but regardless of how he treated her, Devoted's love was relentless. He wasn't used to getting this kind of love, loyalty, and dedication from anyone except for his parents, his brother, and his grandmother. Most other animals he encountered in his life came and went, but Devoted remained committed throughout their time together. Eventually, he realized how lucky he was to have a best friend like her and finally started to understand how truly special their relationship was. Their friendship flourished more and more as time progressed, but Rich was still searching for what eluded him all these years, his true love.

Chapter 2

Ideal Ly, the Dream

Although Rich was happy living the simple life with Devoted by his side, something always seemed to be missing. He never felt like he lived up to his name. Most people think of Rich as a measure of an abundance of monetary items, including himself. One day, Rich noticed the most amazing rainbow after a tumultuous night of storms the previous evening. Entranced by the beauty of its vibrant colors, he suddenly remembered the tale he once heard of what awaits those who find the rainbow's end. If the stories he had been told were true, the ideal and perfect life was a possibility. Rich thought that living happily ever after was finally attainable. All he needed was the glimmer of hope the colorful arch revealed. Without hesitation, he started following the vibrant arc. Will Rich find his "ideal" happiness? Unknowingly, he wandered through an unfamiliar part of the Forest in his quest to make his dream a reality. He kept his head up and his hopes high, unaware of his surroundings. Eventually, he snapped out of his entrancement and realized he had no idea where he was. He felt his heart thumping from within. To make the situation worse, Rich suddenly sensed he was no longer alone as his long ears and keen hearing picked up the sound of danger fast approaching.

Chapter 3

Heinous, Hateful, and Harmful—the Horrible Hyenas

The rustling of the leaves behind Rich seemed to get louder with each passing moment. Between a few of the dense brushes appeared three sets of piercing red eyes. The three pairs of ruby-like peepers belonged to a pack of hyenas that locked onto their prey. Heinous was the oldest hyena and the leader of the group. While most animals hunted for survival, she just loved to hurt and harm things without much reason. Her evil ways knew no bounds, and all she cared about was the power to control. Hateful, the middle brother, has never met another animal that he liked. It was a surprise he was able to tolerate his two siblings for all these years. Harmful is the youngest of the three, had many reckless and radical ideas of changing the Forest for many years, but was completely oblivious to the damage he caused. Between the three siblings, there was a danger spreading through the Friend Ly Forest it had never seen before. Once Rich realized the danger lurking behind, he started hopping faster and faster, looking back at every twist and turn until abruptly he tripped over a rock and went over a cliff and into the water beneath.

Chapter 4

Sneaky and Secretive, the Sharks

As Rich was thrust into the water by his momentum, he became abundantly aware that he never learned how to swim. His sheer exhaustion from escaping his predators gave him no chance to survive the raging river as he sank instantaneously. Rich's struggles to keep his head above water proved futile. As he felt himself taking a last gasp, he suddenly felt a force bringing him toward the clear morning sky. Rich was being lifted from beneath and elevated higher than he had ever been before by a gentle giraffe. Little did Rich and his savior realize that following behind them were the three original predators along with two more vicious allies. His sudden tumble into the water had temporarily prevented the hyenas from following his trail, but they were able to get help from their own friends, Sneaky and Secretive. Sneaky and Secretive are known to conceal themselves and are subtle in their actions, which makes it easy for them to hunt down their prey. Years ago, they made an agreement with the hyenas. The sharks would provide transportation for the hyenas across the water, and in return, the hyenas would deliberately toss in the remains as special snacks for their allies. This partnership has proved to be mutually beneficial through the years. Riding the sharks allowed the hyenas to navigate the turbulent water and continue hunting their prey.

Chapter 5

Genuine Ly, the Giraffe

Once they got across, the long-necked beauty lowered him onto a patch of grass just beyond the sandy beach. She looked gently at him. Kindness emanated from her caring eyes as she also recognized her old friend. They met when Rich helped Genuine with a tooth problem. Rich had a lot of dental problems as a young bunny, so he was able to help her out in her time of need. Now, Genuine Ly was able to return the favor, saving him from death. She inquired about how Rich got himself in such a predicament. He briefly explained how he had wandered away from home chasing a rainbow when he sensed he was being followed and ended up in a full sprint through the Forest that came to an abrupt and unexpected splash. Genuine looked on with concern and gave him a sense of comfort even without words. Suddenly, Rich collapsed, but luckily for him, he was saved by the right animal as she quickly nursed him back to health. It wasn't her long neck but her enormous heart that made her special. She was known throughout the Forest for helping animals of all sizes reach new heights. Her giving nature and true concern for the well-being of others exemplified Genuine perfectly. She intuitively knew that Rich needed more than just physical help. Devoted was the only animal that showed Rich this kind of warmth since he lost his parents years ago. Without Devoted by his side, seeing Genuine again gave him renewed hope. Though he was still weak from all that he endured, Rich willed himself up and told Genuine that he had to go. She encouraged him to stay to make sure he was healthy enough, both physically and mentally, to make his journey home, but he declined and explained that he needed to get back to Devoted Ly. Genuine completely understood as she has a loving family of her own whom she was foraging for when she spotted her drowning friend. Before Rich left, Genuine packed a few extra McIntosh apples for him to bring on his journey home so he had the energy to get back safely. As he left, Rich glanced back at Genuine Ly and hoped he could bring Devoted back someday to meet her. She had a major impact on Rich. Not only had she nursed him back to health physically, she gave him strength emotionally in the form of hope.

Chapter 6

Patient Ly, the Puppy

Patiently waiting for him at home was Devoted Ly as the sun went down and the darkness overtook the night sky. Her concerns for her best friend increased with the illumination of the night sky. Rich has never been gone this long before. Devoted sensed something wasn't right and headed into the depths of the night to find her friend. Little did she expect that it was the beginning of an adventure of a lifetime.

Devoted went to Rich's favorite trail and used her keen sense of smell to pick up her best friend's scent instantaneously. Once she locked onto his scent, she just unwaveringly followed it. Eventually, she became unfamiliar with her surroundings but relentlessly followed Rich's trail until it came to an abrupt end, stopped by a raging river below. Devoted had always been extremely afraid of water, so she paced back and forth trying to figure out what to do. Finally, she knew what had to be done. Without regard for her own safety, Devoted jumped into the water hoping she could doggy-paddle her way to the other side. Unfortunately, once she jumped in, Devoted began to sink immediately and whimpered for help. Suddenly, out of nowhere, a dark shadow came swooping down and grabbed the chubby pooch. Within a few seconds, she was looking at the river from high above and gliding toward the other side. Though she had never seen the world from that vantage point, Devoted never felt so safe. As quickly as she ascended, the decline toward land was just as rapid. Gently, she was placed on a bed of flowers on the other side of the river.

Chapter 7

Fearless Ly, the Dragon

Devoted Ly glanced up and saw a baby golden dragon flapping his tiny multicolored wings. After breathing out a puff of smoke, he asked if Devoted was okay and followed it up in a cute voice. "I'm Fearless Ly, what's your name?" Devoted introduced herself, still gasping for air after expelling the residual water she inhaled in the river. "Why did you jump into the river when clearly you cannot swim?" he asked. "I'm Devoted Ly and I was looking for my best friend and his trail ended at the river," she responded.

Fearless understood right away how his new friend got her name. Her devotion and dedication to her friend was clear. Devoted asked Fearless how he got his name. "My dad gave me the name because he wanted me to be brave and willing to try different things in life without being afraid of failure. The more you experience in life, the more fulfilled you will feel." His dad constantly reminded him, "Never be scared to fail as one learns more from failure than from success. As long as you try your best, there will be no regrets regardless of the outcome."

Devoted liked her new friend and sensed she made another companion for life. She had just fearlessly left her home to look for her best friend, so she fully understood that the best things in life are worth risking everything for. Devoted shook the water off her drenched body and was eager to continue her search. Fearless Ly wanted to ensure Devoted's safety by accompanying her through his home, the Friend Ly Forest, which his dad often referred to as America. So their adventure began together.

Chapter 8

Mother and Father Ly, the Mice and Horses

Searching for Rich was exhilarating for both Devoted and Fearless. As they looked up into the sky, they saw images of their parents in the clouds. Aside from raising them, each of their parents tried to teach them about living life to its fullest. Father Ly and Mother Ly were the common names shared by each of their parents. Although they were completely different species, they inherently possessed similar characteristics as parents. Father and Mother Ly provided love and nurturing for all their children. Generally, parents want to nurture and raise their young to be able to take care of themselves and contribute to society someday. A big part of growing up is being able to make responsible decisions. Hopefully, someday you can also pass the knowledge on to your own offspring. There are many things parents would like to protect their children from and also a few dangers they will never foresee. The only thing that parents can do is provide a safe environment to grow and develop for their children. Remembering the fatherly advice and motherly nurturing they received, Devoted and Fearless Ly soared through the air together, separately but simultaneously realizing how lucky they were to have such great parents. With each flap of Fearless Ly's tiny wings, their trust in each other grew as they ascended into the clouds.

Chapter 9

Bull and Brother and Diligent Ly, the Bulls and Dragon

As Devoted and Fearless descended through the clouds, they saw a clearing ahead with some activity. They approached and watched two big bulls charging toward each other while another creature looked on, which appeared to be a blue dragon. When they heard the winds of change created by Fearless Ly's wings, the bigger bull turned and watched with exuberance as the unusual pair descended. The flying duo came down swiftly, and Fearless flew without hesitation toward the three large beasts. When they landed near the enormous trio, Fearless jubilantly called out to them, "Hi, Uncles and Auntie." It turned out the big three were a part of Fearless's family. The dragon, his auntie, "Diligent" Ly, married Bull Ly. The third creature was Bull's younger sibling, Brother Ly. The two brothers were inseparable growing up and met Fearless's aunt later on in their teenage years. Ironically, Bull Ly was anything but a "bully." In fact, he was the total opposite. He was larger and stronger than his baby brother and found himself always protecting him among others in the Forest. In return, Brother Ly always showed affection and reciprocated his brother's love. For the longest time, the three of them were best friends.

The threesome asked Fearless about his new adorable friend. He quickly filled them in on his devoted friend's search for her long-eared companion. Diligent precisely recalled a tiny bunny being chased by three hyenas through the Forest while she was working hard to provide for her family. Diligent was known throughout the Forest for her great work ethic. By the time she realized what was happening and wanted to help, they disappeared into the depths of the Forest, apparently following the rainbow's path, which disappeared amid the ominous clouds engulfing part of the Forest. Bull, Brother, and Diligent Ly offered to help, but Fearless and Devoted declined, fearing that the bigger group would slow their pursuit. They also saw this as their opportunity to prove themselves. They said their farewells and swiftly headed into the darkening skies ahead.

Chapter 10

Considerate Ly, the Cat

As Rich persevered through the Forest, another memory came to his mind as he approached a range of mountains. Thinking about his Grandma, Considerate Ly, always gave Rich a sense of tranquility. During the earlier years of his life, she helped take care of Rich and his brother. She had such an influence on his development since she took care of the two siblings while their parents were out foraging for food. For many years, she would tell stories that emphasized certain qualities that Rich possessed, which set him apart from his older brother. Although his brother was one of the cutest and funniest animals you could ever meet, there was something that made Rich special too. Though he always seemed to live in his brother's shadow, he possessed an innate quality that allowed Rich to evolve into a unique creature in his own right. His grandma would tell him stories about Rich as a young bunny that reinforced some of his natural inclinations to think of others first. The first involved the scarcity of food they faced as a family growing up. Whenever Rich's dad brought home food for his kids, Rich was hesitant to eat. Somewhat perplexed, his grandma would ask him why he hadn't devoured the treat like his big brother. Bashfully, he would reply, "But what about you, Grandma? I don't want to eat unless you have some too!" This story emphasized Rich's consideration of others. The second tale she would reiterate was one in which Rich would stop playing and run to her whenever she needed to cross the ravine to get food. Inquisitively, she would ask him why. He warmed her heart as he replied, "I just want to make sure you cross over safely first." These two stories Considerate Ly retold helped to reinforce his tendency to think of others first. It reminded him that it was selfish of him to wander off without considering how Devoted would worry about him. It gave him the determination and strength to survive to return home to Devoted Ly.

Chapter 11

Unique Ly, the Unicorn

Devoted and Fearless whisked through the Forest in spite of encountering inclement weather. The storm's blustery winds and piercing rain were not enough to curtail their pursuit. It just increased their determination, persistence, and perseverance. As the dark clouds parted, they saw a beautiful meadow with colorful flowers surrounding the green wild grass, and the rainbow reappeared. They approached the scenic field and landed in the middle when a special white horse glided out of the sky and jumped over them effortlessly. In the middle of her forehead appeared a single golden horn, and she also had a beautiful rainbow-colored mane and wings to match. She was like no other horse Devoted and Fearless had ever seen before. "My name is Unique Ly," the unicorn introduced herself. She was excited to meet her two new friends and asked what their names are. Devoted and Fearless answered, and she loved each of their responses. "Your names are just as unique as mine!" She revealed that because her single horn wasn't always golden and her tiny wings were disproportionate to her body, Unique was once picked on by the other animals. As she matured, her horn changed from a brownish hue to a golden glow. Matching her exquisite horn, the feathers on her tiny wings molted and changed to incorporate the spectrum of the rainbow, and her mane matched its beauty. Since then, she has always embraced not only her unique features but also greatly appreciated the differences in others. They asked if she had seen a bluish gray rabbit recently. She advised them that yesterday, a little bunny scampered through the field apparently being pursued by three vicious, hungry hyenas but appeared to be following the path of the rainbow. Unique pointed them in the right direction and also provided food and nourishment for them prior to their departure. Devoted and Fearless thanked Unique for her care and kindness before they followed the rainbow into the Forest.

Chapter 12

Generous Ly, the German Shepherd

So many animals who affected his life ran through Rich's head as he scurried through the Forest. Another animal was his uncle, Generous Ly. Rich's parents met Generous in their native land when he was on a mission along with his few and proud pack sent to protect against a destructive ideology spreading in a faraway land. Eventually, the assistance no longer was sustainable, and pressures to return home mounted. Rich's family subsequently lost their native land soon afterward. Luckily, they were able to escape and find refuge in Generous Ly's homeland, which soon became their forever home, the Friend Ly Forest. Rich wasn't his given name when he was born. He chose it to honor his Uncle. Generous was extremely giving and helpful when Rich's family were accepted into the Friend Ly Forest. His giving nature showed no bounds as he also helped many other animals he encountered around the Forest throughout his life. Although they were a completely different species, Generous Ly became a significant part of their extended family. Eventually he became the reason Rich chose to change his name. Generous Ly epitomized the giving heart of the Friend Ly Forest. Someday, Rich hoped to grow up to be just like his uncle and adopt his giving ways. He knew his job was not done and wanted to make a difference and give back to his amazing homeland. This gave him even more reason to persevere.

Chapter 13

Tru, Honest, and Sincere Ly—the Tiger, the Horse, and the Snake

Although Devoted was honed in on Rich's trail, she suddenly picked up three other distinctly different scents permeating the fresh crisp air. Trying not to be distracted by the other new scents, she continued to direct Fearless where to fly. Meanwhile, Fearless immensely enjoyed their adventure together. All he knew was that around every tree and over every mountain was a new experience that was truly exhilarating. He was finally experiencing life without fear thanks to his canine friend. When they came to the next clearing, they saw an interesting sight. There were three very different animals chasing each other around. At first glance, it appeared they were attacking each other, which emboldened Fearless to transition into his protective mode. As they approached, he let out a roar, but his warning did little to gain the attention of the three animals. Then, without restraint, he reared back and allowed the ferocious fire to come from deep within. The blaze instantly got the animals' attention as it lit up the baby-blue sky.

The inferno finally stopped the animals in their tracks, and the tiger, Tru Ly, responded first. "If you wanted to play with us, all you had to do was ask. There is no need to set the Forest on fire!"

Fearless looked perplexed and answered, "You guys were just playing?"

In a hissing but sweet genuine voice, the baby snake, Sincere Ly, answered, "Yes, these are my cousins. Can we help you guys?"

Lastly, the tiny horse, Honest Ly, added, "We can assist you if you're lost or need any help."

The three showed their genuine concern for the two strangers and were all raised to be truthful, honest, and sincere, which Devoted and Fearless both greatly appreciated and felt instantly connected to them. They wanted to stay and enjoy the company of their three new friends but knew that time was of the essence to save Rich. Although their encounter was brief, the five knew it wouldn't be the last time they would meet, so they said their goodbyes and continued their quest.

Chapter 14

The Believable Oppressor, Oblivious, and Pernicious—
the Sheep, the Donkey, and the Parrots

As Rich wandered deeper into the Forest, he had now met his share of both good and bad animals, but he still thought as a whole, the rest of the Friend Ly Forest was the most amazing place he has ever been. In the midst of his journey home, he came upon a very different part of the Forest. Rich had never seen such a pristine and immaculate place before. The structures within this section were pure white, which only highlighted the beautifully manicured pink flowering cherry blossom trees. Residing there were predominantly two groups of animals, the elephants to the right and the donkeys on the left. Standing in front of the donkeys was a random sheep and a white mane donkey by his side. Each of them had parrots that stood on their shoulders, ready to echo their bidding. Little did he know, the sheep standing before him was the elected leader of the Forest. He was known as the Believable Oppressor, the first sheep to be the leader of the Friend Ly Forest. Rich was surprised that the leader of the Forest was an animal not known for its power or strength, but it didn't take long for Rich to realize that his prowess was exerted in a different way. He was eloquent and polite, almost to a fault, but convincing to most at first. The sheep told Rich all about this special place, where animals from all over the Forest gathered to create the laws of the land. This location superficially appeared to be one of the purest places, but it was only a facade for one of the filthiest places in the Friend Ly Forest. Likewise, the seemingly benign-looking sheep was one of the most sinister animals in the Forest. He fed on the hope for change within the Forest and utilized his charm and charisma to fool many of the animals he encountered, including Rich, initially. In his vulnerable state, he was offered a safe sanctuary from the dangerous predators on his trail. It turned out that the Believable Oppressor was in essence a wolf in sheep's clothing and the hyenas were a part of his plans to control the Forest. By the time many of the animals realized it, the modifications he made in the once freedom-loving Forest made it harder and harder to recognize. It was a precarious place where all animals looked different but had to think the same. He managed to control their minds under the guise of providing fairness and equality throughout the Forest. Many animals literally followed him like sheep. They spoke under the pretense of care for other animals but secretly were only concerned about their own power and control. By his side was Oblivious, the donkey, who had no clue how the Forest functioned as an ecosystem. To make things worse, the Pernicious Parrots that rode on their shoulders were always ready to repeat their lies throughout the Forest, slowly causing harm to all within its borders. The spread of inaccurate information allowed them to control the other animals through fear and division, but luckily there were still a few animals who wanted to preserve the sanctity of the Friend Ly Forest, which was based on their collective freedoms. Wandering through this part of the Forest would change Rich's perspective on life forever as he started to understand how his family lost their original homeland. It always seems to begin with the benign message of equality for all, but inevitably transforms into an abuse of power. Now, it seemed that history was about to repeat itself. Luckily, a chance encounter with an arctic fox and her baby would help Rich escape the land of lies.

28

Chapter 15

Faithful and Hopeful Ly, the Arctic Fox and Baby Fox

Unaware of what was happening, Rich had been cajoled by the Believable Oppressor and his obsequious band of double talking donkeys under the pretense of aiding him during his greatest time of need. The shelter they offered him was in actuality an invisible cage that kept him captive to become easy prey for the hyenas pursuing him. The system was in place to take advantage of the most vulnerable. Little did they know, Rich's soft exterior hid his true strength within. His mom taught him to beware of false kindness. Snapping him out of his trance was a friendly arctic fox and her baby kit. The fox's stunning beauty was captivating, but it was her sweetness, sincerity, and genuine concern for him that gained his trust. The mama fox said in a caringly calm voice, "Are you okay? I'm Faithful Ly, and this is my baby, Hopeful Ly." Hopeful bashfully hid behind her mom as Faithful told the bunny about how they had come from a faraway land called South Carolina to report news from the rest of the Friend Ly Forest. They were also spreading their hope and faith throughout the Forest along the way. Rich was suddenly reminded of how his mom used to pray for the well-being of her entire family and the Forest. Although he never fully believed in the power of prayer, he found himself intrigued by the purity of love emanating from the two arctic foxes. It was a revelation to Rich when he learned from Faithful the truths about what is happening throughout the Forest. He was unaware of so many of the events in the Forest since he had been so busy most of his life working hard to provide for his family. The Friend Ly Forest had mainly good animals, but some who threatened its sanctity. Not all are as they seem, which Rich almost learned the hard way. Though it is the most amazing place in the world, it is not without its own flaws and issues as sometimes having too much freedom can also cause problems. The fundamentals of what made this place special was being challenged from within. With this new knowledge, Rich was ready to find his way home and hopefully try to defend the land they love against the evil within its borders. Rich had always wanted to give back to the Friend Ly Forest that gave him and his family so much, and now he was inspired by a newfound purpose to survive so that he could repay his debt to his great home, which is being compromised from within. It was obvious that Faithful had seen a lot in her life but somehow remained as hopeful as her daughter's name. Faithful reminded Rich of his dear friend Genuine Ly and gave him renewed hope that he would not only see Devoted one day but also see his long-necked and giant-hearted friend too. Faithful Ly reminded Rich to keep the faith and belief, that there is a reason for everything happening to him, and that good will triumph over evil. With that sentiment, the two beautiful foxes guided Rich back into the right direction of the rainbow.

30

Chapter 16

Persuasive Ly, the Penguin

As Devoted and Fearless left their newfound friends, something felt different. Their senses heightened as it seemed like they were being followed. They checked behind them occasionally but didn't see anything. Devoted could definitely smell the scent of something unusual. Fearless looked down at Devoted and knew what they had to do. They flew around in a circle to see if anyone was following them. That was when they saw movement from behind a pink flowering tree.

Fearless and Devoted simultaneously called out in their toughest voices, "Hey! Come out and show yourself!"

The little penguin peeked out playfully. "Hey, guys, I thought you'd never find me!" he said in the most amicable voice and followed with, "I'm Persuasive, what are your names?"

Both Devoted and Fearless looked curiously at the fluffy little penguin. "Why were you acting so suspiciously!" they said again in sync.

Persuasive answered in a convincing manner, "I'm just looking for new friends to play with."

They gave him a serious stare and responded, "We'd love to stay and play, but we're looking for our best friend!"

In response, Persuasive offered his assistance and explained to his new friends that despite his youth and size, he had been through many adventures in his life already. He is very resilient and a lot tougher than he looks. His articulate voice was extremely convincing and compelling. Devoted and Fearless looked at each other and understood how Persuasive got his name and how he may be able to help in their quest to save their friend. Little did they know, Persuasive had been under the spell of an evil that loomed in the Forest. Was he going to be a help or hindrance in their quest to save their friend? Delightedly, Persuasive was excited to start an adventure with his new friends. The three of them went off swiftly back on Rich's trail.

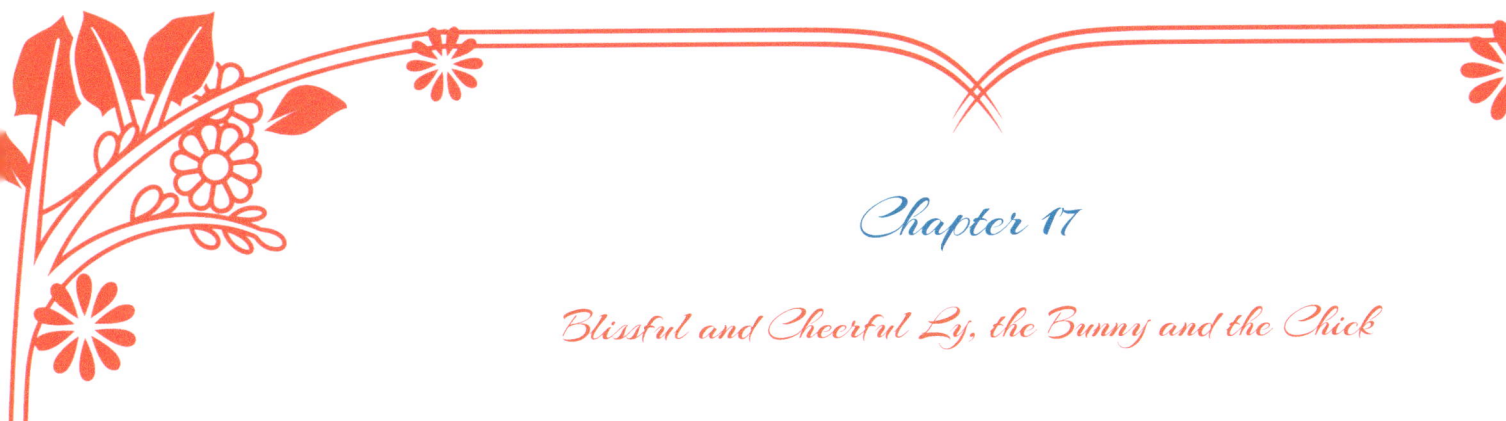

Chapter 17

Blissful and Cheerful Ly, the Bunny and the Chick

The journey Rich has been on has given him a new perspective on his own life. Like all other animals, he has gone through challenges, but overall, he has been blessed by all the amazing animals he's met, both past and present. When Rich's family first arrived in their new home, they had trouble navigating the land and foraging for food because of the tough terrain. They were in a more remote part of the Friend Ly Forest, which made starting a new life more difficult. Rich's dad, Father Ly, had a cousin in the northeast part of the Forest, so the family relocated north. Not only did Rich's extended family help them get settled into another unfamiliar place, his aunt and uncle showed Rich's parents how to forage for survival. In addition, Rich and his older brother were given two younger cousins, who became like their own siblings through the years. In fact, because his female cousin, Blissful Ly, was born in the same year as him, they were like twin cousins. She now has her own daughter, a baby chick named Cheerful Ly. Both Blissful and Cheerful brought another facet of happiness Rich had never experienced before, the love and joy a female's perspective brings. Through the years, Rich had always wondered what true happiness was, which is why he wandered into this predicament. Not only did he have Devoted waiting for him at home, Blissful and Cheerful were among two other loved ones he looked forward to reuniting with when he is able to get home.

Persuasive didn't slow down the determined duo one bit. In fact, he turned out to be full of energy and even led the way for parts of their excursion due to his familiarity with the Forest. Eventually, Rich's trail ended at another shoreline.

As the threesome deliberated on their next step, they suddenly heard a bellowing voice that came from the water. "Son, we were wondering when you would return for dinner," called a huge humpback whale emerging from the ocean. He was accompanied by a smaller black and white orca.

"Hey, Mom and Dad!" Persuasive gleefully called out, hardly able to conceal his excitement to introduce his parents to his new friends. "That's Humble and Kind, my dad and mom."

Devoted and Fearless looked at Persuasive, confused about how he managed to have two whales as parents. Persuasive enthusiastically explained how they became a family. His mom is an orca, better known as a killer whale, which is ironic since she wouldn't harm a fly. She had been known as one of the most caring and compassionate animals throughout the world. In fact, it was Kind who nurtured Persuasive when the penguin egg was washed from the shore into the ocean. Luckily, the little egg floated its way into her blowhole. When she realized what obstructed her airway, she was so excited to bring the blessing to Humble, her love. In spite of his size and strength, Humble never boasted about his power and other abilities. He didn't have an ounce of arrogance in his enormous body. Unfortunately, they were never able to conceive babies of their own, so she knew the tiny egg was their prayers being answered. She also knew Humble would be the perfect father to teach their baby about honor and humility. He not only provided and protected the family and others, he taught Persuasive never to brag about his own capabilities as well. Humble and Kind had always wanted a baby, and Persuasive had made their dreams come true.

"Mom, Dad, did you guys see a blue bunny hop this way?"

Without hesitation, Kind revealed, "Yes, he scurried by yesterday with a pack of hyenas chasing closely behind. He jumped into the water and was rescued by a gorgeous giraffe who brought him to safety on the smaller island. We can show you where they went."

Fearless lifted Devoted and Persuasive, and the three quickly followed Humble and Kind from above.

Chapter 19

Unfortunate Ly, the Fortress

Escaping the heinous hyenas was no easy task, and the grasp of the Believable Oppressor's attempted influence was even more challenging, but thanks to Faithful and Hopeful Ly, he was able to elude capture both physically and mentally. Rich Ly was hungry and exhausted after running for what felt like days without stopping, still following the rainbow's path. Glancing up at the sky, he saw the ominous clouds starting to approach. All he wished for in his delirious state was to find shelter to recuperate. He scurried through this narrow pathway, and suddenly he saw a majestic structure. It was ash gray in color and had sharp angles unlike anything Rich had ever seen before. As he approached, he noticed a moat around the fortress. But instead of alligators or other dangerous animals known to guard the seemingly abandoned castle, the protective barrier was filled with the most beautiful koi fish Rich had ever seen. Aside from their vibrant colors and enormous size, they seemed to welcome Rich as he scurried across the little bridge by jumping out of the water. It appeared that Rich's prayer was answered as this seemed like the perfect sanctuary for some repose and safety. A part of him even thought this could be a permanent residence he can bring Devoted to someday. As Rich entered the structure, he was just as impressed with its unique interior. He found a cozy corner and fell instantly asleep. Little did he know that his initial instincts only gave him a false sense of safety and security. Within hours of him falling asleep, he was rudely awakened by the most horrific of noises, and Rich realized he was not alone.

Chapter 20

Radical and Reckless, the Raccoons

The scratching noises that awakened Rich seemed to be getting louder as it echoed through the premises. Carefully, Rich explored his temporary sanctuary and followed the resonating sounds. Although he didn't see anything, the relentless noise seemed to be coming from high above. The scratching sound that bellowed through the place continued throughout most of the night. Though he was still nervous about the origins of the ruckus, his exhaustion ultimately won out, and he fell into a deep sleep. As the dawn emerged, the sun's rays lit up the fortress and gradually brought Rich out of his somber state. What expedited his revival was the sound of a steady drip of water that rained from multiple areas above. Suddenly, even in his lessened consciousness, he remembered the events of last night. He shook off the residual fatigue and started to clear the fortress again. As he walked by the entranceway, he noticed a big hole from up above that wasn't there the previous evening. That was when he realized that he was no longer alone. Standing in the shadows were two figures. They stepped forward and appeared to be wearing masks around their mostly gray faces. Their striped tails elevated as if they were ready to attack. As they moved closer, Rich noticed one of them making loud noises, similar to those he heard last night. With a warning scowl, she called out to her sister, who could barely refrain from attacking Rich. "Reckless!" she yelled in a loud and disruptive cry. "It's only fair to give the little guy a running start," as she changed the rules of the hunt. Reckless lived up to her name and acted without thinking or caring about the consequences of her actions. Rich saw the perfect potential of his future home quickly disappear. He was blinded by the magnificence of the structure, Unfortunate Ly, but overlooked the dangers of its isolation and seclusion. He instinctively darted out of the entrance and expeditiously hopped past the moat once again. But even in his haste, he could see that the fascinating fish that greeted him yesterday had disappeared. Somehow, he knew it wasn't the last time seeing them.

Chapter 21

Fortunate Ly, the Firebird

Rich Ly overlooked Fortunate Ly, the Firebird, when he rushed into the fortress the previous evening, but she saved him from another set of sadistic strangers. Luck would once again be by his side when it seemed like the end was inevitable. As the reckless raccoons quickly closed in on him, Rich got an unexpected lift from Fortunate, who also helped rescue the koi fish from their captors. From the beginning, he was blessed with the best and most resilient parents during a time of turmoil in his original home. He had an amazing older brother and best friend from the start to share his childhood. After being separated from their parents escaping their old home, they were lucky enough to reunite with them. Their parents survived an ordeal that many hadn't by shear perseverance. Not only was the reunion a sign of good fortune, they became a family again in the land of the free, the Friend Ly Forest. It was a far better place than the place Rich was born. Rich always felt that he was more lucky than good in most situations, almost as if he had a guardian angel protecting him. He often felt undeserving of all his good fortune. He often wondered when his luck would eventually run out. Seemingly, today was not that day as Fortunate Ly allowed him to escape capture once again and live to fight another day. Rich vowed never to forget his good luck and hopefully pay it forward in the future.

Chapter 22

Confident Ly, the Chubby Hamster

Following Rich's trail has been very basic and straightforward once Fearless and Devoted realized his path wasn't just haphazard. It had become clear after the first day that he was following the rainbow up above. Like most parts of life, the youthful partners eventually came to a fork in the road with a big decision to make. Standing in front of the bifid pathway was a fluffy hamster. They made some quick introductions, and he revealed his name, Confident Ly. Knowing that time is of the essence, they struggled to decide which path to take. Confident Ly lived up to his name by reassuring them that regardless of the choice they were about to make, they had to remain self-assured and composed to complete their mission and find their friend. "Not every decision we make in life will lead us to the result we anticipate, so it is up to us to adjust and adapt especially if things do not go our way. Our abilities to work through challenging situations will allow us to build our self-confidence and assurance for future endeavors," he said confidently. Though he was young in age, apparently Confident Ly has experienced life enough to give his new friends the reassurance they needed to continue their pursuit. The consequences of each decision we make in life will be a learning experience that gives us the confidence to choose our paths in the future.

Chapter 23

Sweet and Happi Ly, the Puppy and the Hamster

Although Rich had met some of the most amazing friends during his adventure, he had also encountered some of the most heinous. Through it all, he persevered with the thoughts of how blessed he was to have his family and friends, both past and present. Rich started having a better understanding of why he chose his name. His life was enriched by those who surrounded him since birth, but he never fully appreciated it. Years ago, Devoted started to open Rich's heart with her unconditional love, but it took being separated from his dear friend to make him fully realize the impact she had on his life. He clung on to the fruit from Genuine that he hoped to give to Devoted someday when suddenly he noticed a little brown puff wiggling and wagging its tail. Rich didn't want to disturb him, but something about him felt very familiar. "Excuse me," Rich said. Immediately, the little puff turned around to reveal the cutest puppy face. For a moment, Rich was speechless. Although he was brown in color, he reminded Rich of his best friend. Instantly, he was brought back to the simplicities of their life together. The puppy cleared his throat and introduced himself in the most saccharine voice, "Hey, I'm Sweet Ly, and this is my friend Happi Ly!" He never met Sweet before but felt like he knew him forever. Maybe it was because of his resemblance to Devoted that he gained instant comfort upon meeting Sweet Ly. Even Happi Ly reminded Rich of a childhood hamster friend of his named Joyful Ly. Rich no longer felt lost. Somehow, he knew everything would be okay and he would be reunited with Devoted someday and everything would be okay. Little did he know, Devoted would enrich his life even more with his newfound friends, Fearless and others. Instinctually, Rich extended the apple that his long-necked friend gave him a few days ago. Rich wanted to give it to Devoted when they reunited, but somehow it just felt right to share it with his new friend. In actuality, thinking of Devoted inspired him to instantly offer his new friend the fruit. As he did, Rich also realized that life is meaningless without someone special to share it with. He invited Sweet and Happi Ly to join him on his journey home, and they accepted his invitation.

Chapter 24

Heroical Love Ly, the Health Care Worker

After his last encounter with the racoons, Rich thought he was on his way to safety, but As Rich continued along his venture home, he suddenly found himself laboring to breathe and thought it was from the physical exhaustion of the last few days. Unfortunately, his shortness of breath turned rapidly into feeling like he'd been thrown into an icy pond. His chills changed drastically as now he felt an internal burning sensation. All these different sensations evolved into an ache that ran throughout his body until eventually he went limp. There was no way he could continue as his endurance energy came to an abrupt halt. Little did Rich Ly realize that his unforeseen illness would lead to one of the best encounters of his life. As his eyes began to open, Rich gazed into the most loving eyes he could remember since Devoted. The concern emanating from her glistening eyes also reminded him of his friend, Genuine Ly. It was reassuring, in spite of how he felt physically, to awaken to such concern and compassion. The red cross on the front of her neck was a symbol of her health-care background. His difficulty breathing had subsided somewhat, which allowed him to muster up enough air to ask for her name. Though her given name was Love Ly, she was known throughout the Forest as Heroical Ly. Both names exemplified her perfectly. It is her love and compassion for other animals that fueled her relentless pursuit to help others. She was among a team of search-and-rescue dogs that scoured the Friend Ly Forest looking for animals in need of medical attention. Word of an invisible enemy that came from a foreign land had been spreading like wildfire throughout the Forest. Nothing seemed to scare Heroical Ly regardless of the uncertainty behind the spread of the illness. She persevered through the potential danger and continued to save lives tirelessly. It was no wonder Rich felt so safe in her arms. She proved that superheroes do come in small packages when they have huge hearts.

Chapter 25

Courageous Ly, the Cheetah

As Fearless and Devoted zipped through the Forest, they were nearly stopped in their tracks by a stench that permeated the once fresh air. They looked down and noticed animals of all types laying without movement, with just a few exceptions. One in particular was moving at nearly warp speed from animal to animal, apparently trying to help revive them. Each time she stopped, Fearless got a clear look at the adorable cheetah and felt somehow connected to her. She was unlike any other animal he ever encountered in the Forest as he watched her work dauntlessly to help the fallen animals. Although he didn't want to interrupt her work, he needed to know what happened and how he and Devoted could help. Because of her sheer speed, it was hard to keep up with her, but eventually they did when a surviving animal needed her attention.

"Excuse me, can you tell us your name and what happened to all these animals?" Fearless asked in a concerned tone.

The cheetah caught her breath and replied, "Sorry, there's no time to waste because something is spreading through the Forest faster than I can keep up with. It came on so suddenly and seems to be affecting the older animals. I'm Courageous Ly, by the way."

Instantly, Fearless knew why he felt such a connection with her. Their names are synonymous with each other. Watching her made Fearless understand exactly how she got her name. She was fearless in her efforts to help the other animals with no regard for her own safety. Fearless was always trying to live up to the name his dad gave him and now he knew how to finally do it, thanks to Courageous Ly and her actions. She bravely saved countless animals even when the situation seemed hopeless, exposing herself selflessly. Fearless and Devoted realized that Rich may have also been affected by this invisible enemy, which made them even more eager to help Courageous Ly. They didn't realize she was a part of the team of heroic animals, which included Love Ly, who saved Rich the day before.

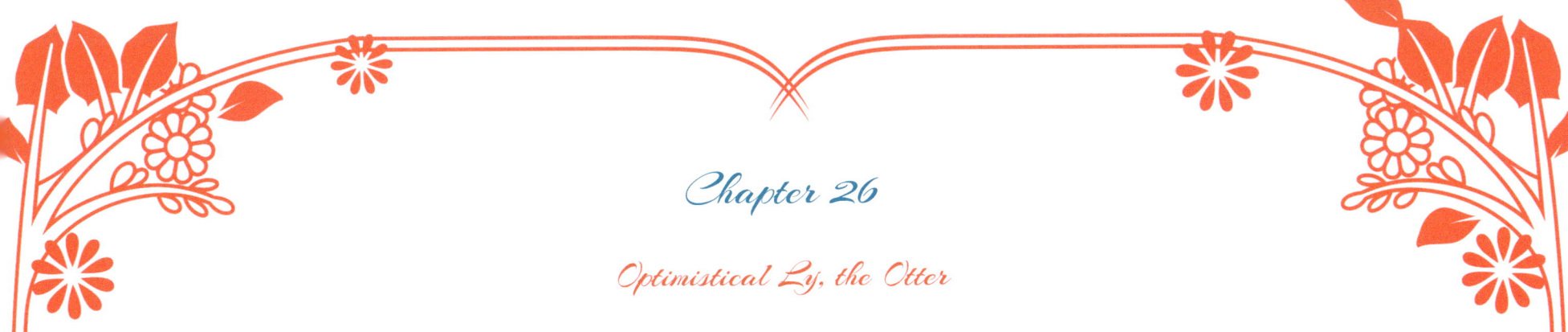

Chapter 26

Optimistical Ly, the Otter

Just when it appeared Devoted and Fearless were gaining ground on their beloved friend, life threw a gigantic obstacle in their way. The early part of their quest was fairly benign. Unfortunately, how quickly the tides changed. Based on what they observed and what their new friend Courageous Ly told them, there appeared to be an outbreak affecting the entire Friend Ly Forest and beyond. As they followed her, they found themselves hoping the next animal she tried to revive wasn't their dear friend. Eventually, they saw enough deceased animals to dampen their hopes of finding Rich alive. They began to have an increasingly pessimistic view on where the path was leading, until they came upon a small ravine. As they approached, a sea otter popped out of the water, surprising them. Though he was reserved in his demeanor, the otter seemed to have a brightness about him and the teddy bear-like baby he was holding. The scene was grim, and he had full awareness of the invisible killer spreading throughout the Forest when the otter, Optimistical Ly, said, "It's always darkest before the dawn! This too shall pass. Adversity builds character. What doesn't kill you will make you stronger." The brief but effective statements gave Devoted, Fearless, and Courageous the lift in their spirits at an opportune time. The positive perspective Optimistical Ly projected was uplifting enough to get them through the toughest of times. This was their opportunity to not only save Rich but also preserve the future of the Friend Ly Forest.

Following the rainbow eventually led Rich, Sweet, Heroical, and Fortunate Ly to what appeared to be a pot of gold surrounded by a backdrop of perfection up in the clouds. Rich didn't know whether he was just delirious from the previous struggles for survival or if what he saw was real. At that moment, he realized that the riches didn't make him any happier. Although Rich met some of the most amazing friends during his adventure, he also encountered some of the most heinous. Through it all, he persevered with the thoughts of how blessed he was to have his family and friends, both past and present. Years ago, something built a wall around Rich's heart, but Devoted started to reopen it with her unconditional love, but it took being separated from his dear friend to make him fully realize the impact she had on his life. All he wanted was to see Devoted again and introduce her to his newfound friends. He reflected on what prompted his journey, chasing a rainbow with the naive belief that it would make him happy. Ironically, it did, but not in the way he expected. It just gave him a better perspective and allowed him to have a newfound appreciation for how blessed his life truly was. His adventure enlightened and enriched him in a much different way by changing his perspective. Although he hadn't done it for years, since his mom passed away, Rich prayed for the chance to see Devoted again internally. He lost his faith years ago when he first lost his dad, wondering how his mom continued to stay so faithful despite suffering the worst loss of her life. Suddenly, he understood why as his prayers were answered when he heard the sweet sound of a familiar bark. He felt like he was dreaming as he saw Devoted camouflaged as a white fluffy cloud and started racing toward him, chasing away the darkness. Without hesitation, he quickly reciprocated her approach and hopped toward her. Once again, Devoted showered Rich with her loving licks. Spontaneously, Rich's eyes welted up, and his tears flowed, full of joy. Once they completed their embrace, they added to their jubilance by mutually introducing each other to their newfound friends. The pot of gold Rich initially thought was at the end of the rainbow was the golden dragon who would change Rich's life forever. Little did they know, their joyful reunion would be short-lived as among them was a friend who had already been brainwashed by the destructive donkeys. Will he lead to their ultimate demise, or would Rich and his friends be able to help save him along with the Friend Ly Forest?

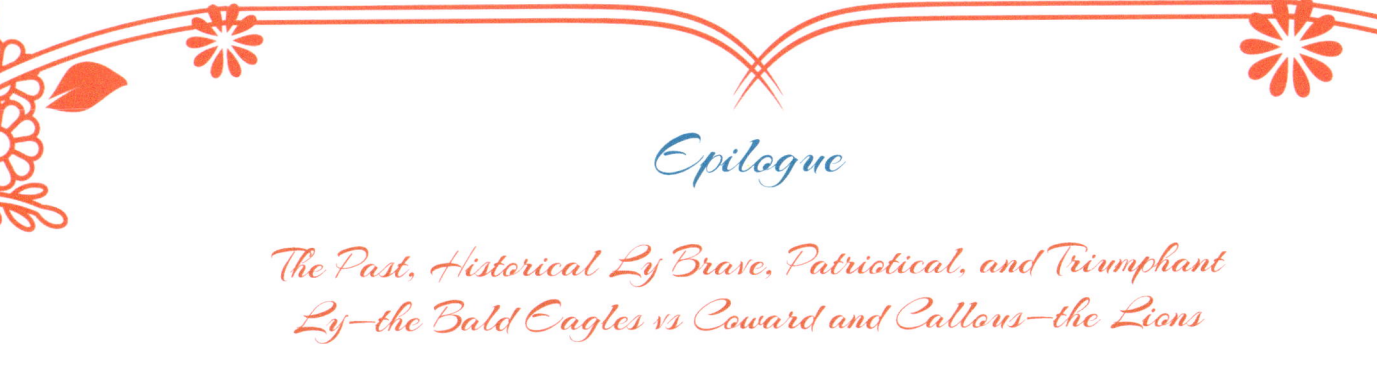

Epilogue

The Past, Historical Ly Brave, Patriotical, and Triumphant Ly—the Bald Eagles vs Coward and Callous—the Lions

So far, their adventure through the Friend Ly Forest has been exciting and fun in spite of the gravity of the situation. Meeting all the different animals was the highlight of the journey. Little did they know, the land they were going through wasn't always so free. It was once ruled by Coward, the lion, a self-proclaimed "King of the Jungle." He reigned over the other animals sheerly because of his size. Living in his kingdom, the animals were never allowed to live freely, until one day a group of animals led by a family of bald eagles decided to fight for their collective freedoms. The leader of the pack, Brave Ly, the bald eagle, believed that all animals in the Forest should have the freedom to raise their young without being oppressed by Coward. Along with his brother, Patriotical Ly, they led the other animals in their fight for freedom. Although many animals were lost during the conflict, it was worth it in the end when they overthrew the lion's regime. Since then, there have been other conflicts that shaped and improved the freedoms in the Forest for all, equally. It made the Friend Ly Forest a place like no other. When word got out about this land of freedom, different animals from other lands journeyed from afar to inhabit this unique land, including Rich's parents. Their physical differences no longer mattered in this special place since they shared a common bond, the belief that all animals were created equal and should share the same freedoms. Recently, the greatness of the Friend "Ly" Forest has been questioned by the resurgence of Coward and one of his cousins, Callous, in an effort to regain their tyrannical rule. Although they were larger than the other animals, their real strength was the cunning and deceitful influence of their donkey friends. They felt that spreading chaos throughout the Forest would give themselves the best opportunity to regain control of the Forest. They caused unrest throughout the Forest, until a huge elephant came along, Donald Triumphant Ly. For years, Triumphant befriended the donkeys but realized the Forest he loved was being destroyed from within by their reckless ideology. The freedoms that all animals were afforded in this great place were being jeopardized by the donkeys' desire to control the Forest. It was because of his love for the Forest that he stepped forward to fight against the lions' and donkeys' attempted takeover. Triumphant was known for his winning ways and loud bellows through his truthful trunk. Though some animals couldn't handle the brutally honest message the elephant echoed because of their heightened sensitivities, most understood that he was standing up for the smaller animals who had no voice and the freedoms they enjoyed. He stood in front to shield many animals from the attacks by Coward, Callous, and their evil allies, which included the hyenas, raccoons, wolves, sheep, parrots, penguins, and sharks, among others. Sadly, about half of the animals in the Forest were fooled by these animals. The propaganda parrots controlled the message spread in the Forest with mostly false narratives from those trying to control it and the animals within. Their strategy to divide and conquer has been going on for years and continued to work. The chaos eventually led to the rise of another hero, Electrical Muscular Ly.

The Present

Valiant, Protective, Lawful, Selfless, and Dutiful Ly

It turned out that reuniting with Devoted and meeting their new friends wasn't the end of their journey, but just the beginning. Rich's adventure through the Friend Ly Forest taught him several lessons. Not only did he learn to appreciate the blessings in his life, he realized the dangers that threaten to take them away. Although most animals came to the Friend "Ly" Forest for freedom, it wasn't always the case for every animal. Some struggled to gain the same freedoms enjoyed by others, but the Forest continues to improve. For years, inequality was a part of the land, but major changes developed through the years as the animals realized that all the animals contribute differently but significantly to keeping the ecosystem of the Forest healthy and strong. Ironically, many animals will never fully appreciate how fortunate they are to be born in the land of the free, while tremendous numbers of animals from foreign lands are still risking everything to come to the Friend Ly Forest. Most animals realized that having peace and prosperity in the Forest requires a semblance of law and order. The animals agreed to a set of rules to protect animals against each other, especially the most vulnerable against the aggressors. They decided to have a protective force within the Forest. Among them were Valiant, Protective, Lawful, Selfless, and Dutiful Ly. These were the animals entrusted to not only enforce the rules of the land but also to ensure the safety of those within it. They were the first to respond when any dangers in the Forest ensued. Unfortunately, due to the history of inequality, the protection under these laws were not always equitable. There were many parts of the Forest where the animals struggled to benefit from the freedoms the Forest provided due to a scarcity of food. The lions, hyenas, raccoons, and donkeys controlled the animals in the inner parts of the Forest by giving morsels of the food they collected from the other animals. They knew they would have the support of these animals by giving them free food and shelter. Although they had an easy life, it prevented them from achieving their full potential. The frustrations of being in an environment lacking any ability to grow made the inner parts of the Forest increasingly more dangerous. The animals often fought each other to survive in that environment, breaking many of the rules established in the Forest. In order to prevent the struggles from escalating, the protective measures in the inner parts of the Forest often have tougher encounters and greater consequences. The team assembled to protect and serve had their hands full.

Valiant, Protective, Lawful, Selfless, and Dutiful Ly were just a handful of animals that police the Forest and keep it safe for the other animals to live. Each of them possessed qualities that were shared by the entire group. Valiant Ly led the group as he was the bravest of the brave and would risk his own safety regardless of the circumstances. Protective Ly prided himself on keeping others safe and even used his own body to shield others from harm. Lawful Ly fully understood the rules of the Forest and made sure to enforce them. Selfless Ly epitomized the animal that would give the fur off his back for any animal he encountered regardless of how it affected her. Dutiful Ly understood the responsibilities entrusted to them by the Forest communities and made sure the job was done effectively and properly. These brothers and sisters in arms served to keep the Forest as peaceful as possible. Recently, there has been unrest in the Forest as there was news throughout the Forest that some of the animals were not being treated fairly. Although most of the first responders served honorably, there were occasionally a few bad ones that abused their powers. These few bad apples were enough to tarnish the reputations of the predominantly good group. The bad animals began to rise up against them and started to destroy the Forest from within. In spite of the loss of respect, many of them continued to protect their respective communities. The law-abiding animals of the Forest continued to support those protecting their homeland from within. They were the thin blue and red lines preventing anarchy, destruction, and chaos from spreading throughout the Forest. Though they were under appreciated for their valor and sacrifice, they persevered to do their jobs effectively.

The Future

Michael Inspirational "Great" Ly, the GOAT

Growing up, Fearless Ly's dad always admired the skills and talents of the most athletic animals in the Forest. One animal in particular was the most inspirational to him and many others, "Great" Ly. The goat was a legend known throughout the Forest for his victories against every animal who challenged him to a jumping contest. In the pinnacle of his greatness, he had reached heights never seen by the other animals that did not possess wings. As the legend of his unique abilities grew, most never realized what it took to get him to the level of near perfection. Fearless's father told him the story from a different perspective. He would emphasize to Fearless that although the goat was born with some unique skills, he was initially smaller than the other animals, which put him at quite a disadvantage. When he tried to play with the other animals, they excluded him because he wasn't good enough. Great Ly began practicing harder and even had a growth spurt to complement his increasing abilities. Eventually, Great was good enough to make the team. Once he accomplished that goal, it gave him the confidence and encouragement to improve. Every time Great was challenged by another animal and was defeated, he used it as a learning experience and challenged himself to work tirelessly on his weaknesses. Most animals were concerned about the embarrassment and ridicule that came with failure, but he used it as motivation to become better. Aspiring to new heights wasn't always easy, but his perseverance continued to set him apart from all the other animals. He led by example through his diligence and persistence. Great wasn't born with this name, but his excellence was developed and fostered by his sheer determination and will through all the trials and tribulations he encountered. That was the moral of Great Ly's story Fearless's father emphasized. His legendary life wasn't seen through the lens as just his successes, but as a reflection of the obstacles he overcame to become the best. Of all his victories, his greatest conquest was winning the battle against cancer, which had taken two of Fearless's grandparents' lives along with many others. Fearless's father wished he challenged himself more in life so that he would have no regrets and wonders of what he could have accomplished. He also understood the greatest growth came from the experiences of failure. Now, Fearless would use Great Ly's inspirational tale to hopefully find Devoted's best friend.

And Beyond

Electrical Muscular Ly, the Electric Eel

Just when Rich and Devoted were finally reunited and introduced to their new friends, they started to realize their journey together was just beginning. Although the Friend Ly Forest had only been around for nearly 250 years, the world as they knew it had been around much longer. As the population of the animals grew, not only in their homeland but also abroad, there have been significant changes, both good and bad. The freedoms the Forest afforded all animals gave most animals the opportunities to thrive and contribute to the growth of the land. Word had gotten around the rest of the world, and other animals started to migrate to this truly unique place. As the populations grew throughout the world, there were noticeable changes in the land they roamed, the water they drank, and even the air they breathed. Luckily, there was an extremely intelligent animal who figured out how to lessen the impact of the developing populations on their environments. Electrical Muscular Ly, an electric eel, figured out a way to help. The electrical current that ran through the synapses of his body and brain created the idea to lessen their negative impact on the world. The electric energy he exuded allowed the animals to move throughout the Forest Ly Forest and beyond without damaging their world as much. His positive influence on the world they live in became more and more popular. His foresight into the needs of the world went even beyond his initial idea. He had a multitude of ideas to revolutionize the world. As he was developing these amazing ideas, he started to notice a negative trend in the Friend Ly Forest, which seemed less and less amicable and friendly. The freedoms that made the Forest unique were noticeably starting to wither away, especially the freedom to speak one's thoughts. The ability to disseminate information and exchange different ideas was drastically disappearing. Only one side of the conversation was being heard, and the control of information was also one-sided. Electrical Muscular Ly flexed his most impactful muscle once again and spoke his mind in spite of the expected retribution. His strength and courage knows no bounds as he knew this battle may even be more important for the world's future. Fearless, Rich, Devoted, Sweet, Heroical, Courageous, and the rest of the God Ly animals were ready for their greatest challenge, following a new leader to save not only the Friend Ly Forest but also the Wonderful World they lived in.

About the Authors

Born on February 21, 1975, in Vietnam and given the name Uy-Tri Ly, Rick was lucky enough to escape the fallen country along with his big brother Uy-Nhung Ly as toddlers, separated from their parents Linh Dao and Ve-Dan Ly for nearly a year. They were finally reunited with their parents in Texas in 1978 largely due to the help of their aunts who already immigrated to the USA. After getting his citizenship, Uy-Tri formally changed his name to Richard Uy-Tri Ly, honoring his Uncle Richard, a US Marine who met his parents during his tour of duty in Vietnam and has been an influential figure in his family since. Richard prefers to be called "Rick" by all his friends and family. Currently, he is a proud US Army Reserve Dental Officer and has honorably served our country since 1994 when he first enlisted as an army medic. In his other professional life, Rick is a general dentist practicing in Suffolk County, Long Island for Gentle Dental by Dental365. His coauthor and son, Brandon Daniel, "Fearless" Ly, was born on July 16, 2012, and changed Rick's life forever. Not only is he the best son Rick could ever have hoped for, he is also the main inspiration behind their children's book, along with honoring his grandparents and their great country, the United States of America. Brandon is currently entering the fifth grade and loves sports, especially baseball and hockey, but spends most of his free time playing Roblox. More importantly, he represents the next generation of proud patriots who love their country. This book emphasizes some of the amazing people who have significant impact on their lives, including one of the featured animals in their book inspired by Adelaide "Courageous" Ewing, who also helped Brandon with a few of the illustrations in *The Friend "Ly" Forest*.

Blurb

The Friend "Ly" Forest: An American Adventure in Adverbs and Adjectives represents our journey through this great country and all the incredible animals we meet along the way. What starts out as a rabbit, "Rich" Ly, chasing a dream and losing his way but eventually learning to appreciate the life he left behind, following the rainbow in hopes of a better life without realizing how great his life already was back home with his best friend, "Devoted" Ly, he realizes very quickly that the grass is not always greener on the other side. Along his adventure to get back home, Rich not only meets the best of what the Forest has to offer, but also the worst. Luckily, his faithful friend, Devoted, is hot on his trail with her relentless pursuit to save him from the dangers and temptations of the Forest. In her quest to rescue her companion, she meets "Fearless" Ly, the baby dragon, and together they have an adventure of a lifetime. Not only do they conquer personal fears, building trust along the way with all the challenges they encounter. Will the lifelong companions be reunited before it's too late, or is this just the beginning of the story?